Nita Mehta's CHINESE cookery

Nita Mehta

B.Sc. (Home Science), M.Sc. (Food and Nutrition), Gold Medalist

co-author
Tanya Mehta

SNAB
Publishers Pvt Ltd

Nita Mehta's
CHINESE
cookery

© Copyright 2002-2003 **SNAB** Publishers Pvt Ltd

WORLD RIGHTS RESERVED. The contents—all recipes, photographs and drawings are original and copyrighted. No portion of this book shall be reproduced, stored in a retrieval system or transmitted by any means, electronic, mechanical, photocopying, recording or otherwise, without the written permission of the publishers.

While every precaution is taken in the preparation of this book, the publisher and the author assume no responsibility for errors or omissions. Neither is any liability assumed for damages resulting from the use of information contained herein.

TRADEMARKS ACKNOWLEDGED. Trademarks used, if any, are acknowledged as trademarks of their respective owners. These are used as reference only and no trademark infringement is intended upon.

Reprint 2003
ISBN 81-7869-020-9

Food Styling and Photography: **SNAB**

Layout and laser typesetting:

N.I.T.A.
☎ 23252948
National Information Technology Academy
3A/3, Asaf Ali Road
New Delhi-110002

Published by:

SNAB
Publishers Pvt. Ltd.
3A/3 Asaf Ali Road,
New Delhi - 110002
Tel: 23252948, 23250091
Telefax: 91-11-23250091

Editorial and Marketing office:
E-348, Greater Kailash-II, N.Delhi-48
Fax: 91-11-26235218 *Tel:* 91-11-26214011, 26238727
E-Mail: nitamehta@email.com
snab@snabindia.com
Website: http://www.nitamehta.com
Website: http://www.snabindia.com

Distributed by:

THE VARIETY BOOK DEPOT
A.V.G. Bhavan, M 3 Con Circus,
New Delhi - 110 001
Tel : 23417175, 23412567; Fax : 23415335

Printed by:

THOMSON PRESS (INDIA) LIMITED

Rs. 89/-

Introduction

This is a complete book on Chinese cuisine ranging from starters to soups, the main course and also some exotic desserts to round off the meal. This book contains recipes of chicken, lamb, seafood and vegetables, all cooked in the Chinese style.

In Chinese cooking, the preparation is of great importance. Many dishes require very fine chopping or shredding of the various ingredients and are combined in a very orderly manner. The main cooking technique used is stir frying. A wok is ideal for this. Never over cook as this will destroy the flavour and crispness of the food.

The recipes given in this book are quick and simple to prepare and all the ingredients used are easily available. Enjoy the taste of China!

Nita Mehta

Contents

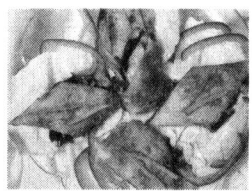

Introduction 5
Important Tips 9
Ingredients for Chinese Dishes 11
Chinese Cooking Methods 14

Starters 17

VEGETARIAN

Honey Chilli Lotus Stem 22
Chilli Paneer with Peppers 26
Spring Rolls 28
Vegetable Gold Coin 32

NON-VEGETARIAN

Golden Fried Prawns 18
Shredded Sesame Chicken 21
Chicken Dim Sums 24
Chicken Spring Rolls 31

Soups 34

VEGETARIAN

Vegetable Stock for Soups 35
Hot & Sour Vegetable Soup 40

NON-VEGETARIAN

Chicken Stock for Soups 36
Hot & Sour Chicken Soup 37

Vegetable Sweet Corn Soup 42 Sweet Corn Chicken Soup 44
Chicken Talumein Soup 46

Chicken, Fish & Mutton Recipes 47

Chicken in Black Pepper Sauce 48
Chicken in Hot Garlic Sauce 50
Chicken Manchurian 52
Spicy Honey Chicken 54
Crispy Fried Fish 56
Dry Chilli Chicken 59
Pork or Mince Meat Balls 60
Mongolian Chicken 62
Honeyed Shrimps 64

Vegetable Dishes 65

Vegetables in Ginger Garlic Sauce with Sesame Seeds 66
Cubed Paneer & Veg. Sizzler 68
Spicy Honey Vegetables 71
Vegetable Manchurian 73
Baby Corns in Ginger Sauce 76
Cantonese Vegetables 78
Vegetable HongKong with Fried Noodles 80

Rice & Noodles 82

VEGETARIAN

Vegetable Fried Rice 83
Haka Noodles with Vegetables 84
American Chopsuey 88
Vegetable Chow Mein 90

NON-VEGETARIAN

Chicken Fried Rice 86
Chicken Haka Noodles 92
American Chicken Chopsuey 95

Desserts 97

Toffee Apples 98
Date & Coconut Pancakes 100

Almond Float 102

Important Tips

- A Chinese dish will have all the vegetables and meat cut in the same shape, e.g. to prepare any dish with noodles, all the vegetables and chicken are always cut into thin long strips. For fried rice, everything is diced — cut into small squares.
- Chinese food is crunchy and full of flavour, so never over cook food.
- Always use a big pan or wok to stir-fry. This avoids mashing or breaking the food into bits.
- Use ajinomoto, the Chinese salt, sparingly. Usually just a pinch is enough. When you double the quantity of the dish, do not double the quantity of ajinomoto.
- The amount of soya sauce can be increased or reduced according to the desired colour of the dish. Remember, soya sauce is salty, so keep a check on the salt when you increase the quantity of soya sauce.
- An important tip while preparing chicken soup is that the stock used must always be prepared by boiling chicken with an onion in water.

- Meat used should be of the highest quality.
- Fish used should always be fresh. Ginger and garlic are invariably used in cooking most fish as this helps a great deal in eliminating the so called fishy smell.
- Young birds should be bought when chicken is used, as the cooking time is usually short. Chicken stock is used in almost all the non vegetarian dishes in place of water.
- Rice or noodles form the staple food of the Chinese. Long grained rice is preferred. Always add noodles or rice to boiling water. When rice is cooked, drain the rice and cool before making fried rice. Noodles when cooked should be drained and washed under running tap water. Rub oil over the noodles so that they don't stick to each other.
- Always serve green chillies in vinegar and chilli sauce as accompaniments with the food.

Ingredients for Chinese Dishes

Bean Sprouts: These are shoots of moong beans or soya beans. The texture is crisp. Bean sprouts are a rich source of vitamins and minerals. To make bean sprouts at home, soak ½ cup of green beans (saboot moong dal) for about 8 hours. Discard water and tie in a muslin cloth. Keep them tied for 2-3 days, remembering to wet the cloth each day. When the shoots are long enough, wash carefully in water. Fresh bean sprouts will keep for several days if refrigerated in a perforated plastic bag.

Chilli Oil: Can be bought ready-made. It can also be made by putting 2 tbsp of chilli powder in a cup and pouring heated oil over it. Use the oil that floats on top.

Chilli Sauce: This is a hot, spicy and tangy sauce made from chillies and vinegar.

Chinese Wine: There are many kinds of wine made from rice. Chinese wine can be substituted by ordinary dry sherry.

Agar-Agar: This is a dried seaweed. The white fibrous strands require soaking and are used like gelatine. It is used for puddings and as a setting agent.

Cornflour: This is used to thicken sauces. Dissolve some cornflour in little water to make a paste and add it to the boiling liquid. Remember to stir the sauce continuously, when the cornflour paste is being added.

Ajinomoto (Monosodium Glutamate): A white crystalline substance commonly known as MSG. It is used in Chinese cooking for enhancing the flavour of dishes. Use it sparingly as it is not considered good for health.

Mushrooms: Both dry and fresh varieties are used in Chinese cooking. To prepare dried mushrooms, soak them in hot water for ½ hour to soften.

Bamboo Shoots: Fresh tender shoots of bamboo plant are available rarely, but tinned bamboo shoots are easily available in the big stores.

Bean Curd or Tofu: Bean Curd or Tofu is prepared from soya bean milk and resembles the Indian Paneer in taste and looks. I have thus substituted it with paneer to give you a few exciting delicacies.

Noodles: Dried thin ad thick noodles are made with and without eggs. They are usually cooked in boiling water till just done, before frying. Never overcook the noodles. Some varieties of rice noodles are simply soaked in warm water till soft & then stir fried.

Sesame Oil: An aromatic oil produced from sesame seeds *(til ka tel)*. Adds flavour to dips, sauces, salads and soups.

Soya Sauce: There are two kinds. One is dark and the other is light. Both are used for flavouring soups, stir fried dishes and for seasoning all Chinese foods.

Spring Onions: These are sometimes called scallions or green onions and are used extensively in Chinese cooking. The green part is also used for garnishing.

Vinegar: Chinese vinegars are made from fermented rice.

Chinese Cooking Methods

PARBOILING:
Parboiling is used when cooking ingredients differ in tenderness and texture. The tougher varieties are added to boiling stock or water for a short time. They are then refreshed in iced water to set color and prevent overcooking. When the parboiled foods are cooked with more tender raw ingredients, the cooking time will then be the same. Whole carrots are peeled, beans are threaded and dropped in boiling water for ½ minute to parboil them. They are then cooled and cut into desired shapes.

STIR-FRYING:
Stir frying food, is to cook food on a high flame for a short period, **stirring continuously.** Ingredients are added to the wok in order of texture and cooking time. Stir frying of vegetables is done in sequence of their tenderness. E.g. onions are stir fried first, then french beans, then carrots, cabbage and so on. Each vegetable is stir fried for a few seconds, before adding the next

vegetable. Ajinomoto is added during stir frying, as it helps to cook the vegetables faster, thus keeping the vegetables crunchy. Stir-frying requires good temperature control and is easily learned through practice. The heat should be progressively raised for the addition of other ingredients. This is used for tender cuts of pork, poultry, seafood and vegetables. The ingredients are sliced, shredded, diced or minced, then stir fried in a wok using a spatula. Before you start stir-frying, remember to --

- ♦ Collect all ingredients required for the recipe.
- ♦ Slice meat, poultry and seafood. Arrange in order of cooking. Marinade food if required, well in time.
- ♦ Measure liquids like oil, sauces and stocks.
- ♦ Blend any thickening agent with stock or water and stir before adding to the wok.

Deep Frying:

Ingredients are cut into even-sized pieces and dipped into a batter such as flour, beaten egg or bread crumbs. These are immersed in hot oil to cover, until cooked.

- A slice of ginger can be added to indicate the oil's temperature for deep frying. If the ginger turns golden, the oil is right for deep frying.
- Marinated ingredients should be drained before dipping into batter for frying.
- Add small quantities of ingredients to the oil at one time. This maintains the oil's temperature.
- Add some fresh oil to used oil before reusing. This prevents oil from discolouring.

Green Chillies in Vinegar

Makes ¼ cup

¼ cup white vinegar, ½ tsp salt, ½ tsp sugar
2-3 drops soya sauce, 2-3 green chillies

1. Chop green chillies finely.
2. Mix all the other ingredients. Add green chillies.
3. Heat on fire till it is just about to boil. Remove from fire. Serve.

Starters

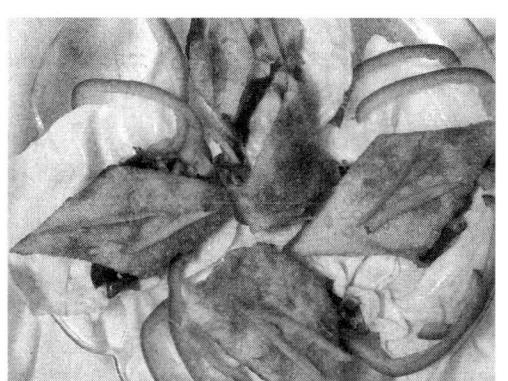

Golden Fried Prawns

Picture on facing page   *Serves 4*

(250 gms) 12 large prawns - cleaned & deveined
1 tbsp sesame seeds (til)

MARINADE
1 tbsp soya sauce
1 tbsp wine or sherry
¼ tsp ajinomoto (optional)
½ tsp salt
¼ tsp black pepper

BATTER
1 egg
3 tbsp plain flour (maida) , 3 tbsp cornflour
3/4 tsp baking powder
1 tbsp oil
¼ tsp white pepper, ¼ tsp salt, ¼ tsp ajinomoto (optional)

1. In a bowl mix soya sauce, sherry, ajinomoto, salt and black pepper. Marinate the prawns in it for 15-30 minutes.
2. Make a smooth paste by adding plain flour, cornflour, baking powder, oil, salt, white pepper and ajinomoto to the egg. Add just enough water to get a very thick batter such that it is of a coating consistency.
3. Dip the prawns into the batter.
4. Sprinkle sesame seeds on the prawns and deep fry one to two pieces at a time, till golden brown.
5. Serve hot with chilli sauce.

Note: If desired you can let the oil remain and then marinate the prawns.

Shredded Sesame Chicken

Picture on cover *Serves 4*

2 chicken breasts, 2 flakes garlic - crushed
1 egg, 4 tbsp cornflour, 1 tbsp soya sauce
1 tbsp sesame seeds (white til), 1 tbsp hot oil, ½ tsp salt and ¼ tsp pepper
¼ of a cabbage - cut into 1" squares, 1 big onion - cut into 8 pieces
2 tbsp oil, 1 tsp ginger-garlic paste, 1½ tsp sesame seeeds
½ tsp vinegar, 1 tbsp soya sauce, 1½ tbsp tomato sauce
½ tsp salt, ¼ tsp pepper, ¼ tsp ajinomoto

1. Boil chicken breasts in ½ cup water with ½ tsp salt and crushed garlic for about 5 minutes or pressure-cook till 1 whistle.
2. Prepare a coating batter with egg, cornflour, soya sauce and sesame seeds. Add 1 tbsp hot oil to the batter. Pat the boiled breasts on a clean napkin. Dip in the prepared batter and shallow fry in a pan in 3 tbsp oil till golden. Remove on paper napkin. Cut into ¾" strips.
3. Heat oil. Add 1½ tsp sesame seeds. Add ginger-garlic paste and onions. Add cabbage. Add all other ingredients. Mix. Add chicken. Mix well.

Honey Chilli Lotus Stem

Picture on page 1   *Serves 4*

200 gm lotus stem (Bhein) - peeled & cut into paper thin slices
2 spring onions - cut white part into rings and greens into 1" pieces
(keep greens separate)
1 tbsp soya sauce
1½ tbsp tomato ketchup, 1 tbsp red chilli sauce
½ tbsp vinegar
1-2 green chillies - chopped finely
4-5 flakes garlic - crushed (optional)
1 tbsp honey
1 tbsp coriander - chopped
¼ tsp each of ajinomoto, salt, pepper, sugar (optional)

BATTER
4 tbsp cornflour, 4 tbsp plain flour (maida)
½ tsp salt, ¼ tsp pepper
2 flakes garlic - crushed to a paste

1. To parboil lotus stem, boil 4 cups water with 1 tsp salt. Add sliced lotus stem to boiling water. Boil for 2 minutes. Strain. Refresh in cold water. Strain and keep aside.
2. Mix plain flour, cornflour, garlic, salt and pepper. Add just enough water, to make a batter of a thick coating consistency, such that it coats the slices of lotus stem.
3. Wipe dry the vegetable with a clean kitchen towel. Dip each piece in batter. Deep fry in two batches to a golden yellow colour. Keep aside.
4. Heat 2 tbsp oil in pan. Reduce heat. Fry the green chillies and garlic till garlic just starts to change colour. Add white of spring onions. Add salt, sugar, pepper and ajinomoto.
5. Reduce heat. Add soya sauce, chilli sauce, tomato ketchup, red chilli sauce and vinegar, stir.
6. Add greens of spring onion. Stir for few seconds.
7. Add honey and mix.
8. Add fried lotus stem and coriander. Mix well till dry and the sauce coats the lotus stem. Remove from heat. Serve hot.

Chicken Dim Sums

Picture on page 2   *Makes 14 pieces*

STUFFING

200 gms chicken mince
2 tbsp very finely chopped onion
1 tbsp chopped parsely or coriander
¼ cup finely chopped carrot
salt & pepper to taste, ½ tsp ajinomoto (optional)
1 tsp soya sauce
2 tbsp oil

DOUGH

1 cup plain flour *(maida)*, 1 tbsp oil, ¼ tsp salt

DIP SAUCE

5 tbsp soya sauce, 2 tbsp white vinegar, 1 tbsp oil
4 flakes garlic - crushed to a paste, ½ tsp chilli powder, 1 tsp tomato ketchup

1. Sift maida with salt. Add oil and knead with enough water to a stiff dough of rolling consistency, as that for puris. Keep in a cool place covered with a damp cloth for 30 minutes.
2. Wash and strain the mince. Press to squeeze out the excess water. Add salt, pepper and oil and churn in a mixer grinder till the mince is very finely ground. Add onion, carrot and parsley. Keep stuffing aside.
3. Take out the dough and form small balls. Roll out flat, as thin as possible into small rounds of 2½" diameter.
4. Put some stuffing in the centre and make it into a balls. Roll the ball between the hands to give it an elongated shape like a roll.
5. To steam, put them in idlis stands or a steamer & steam for 10 minutes.
6. Cool the dim-sums. Cut a slice from the top to expose the filling. Dot with chilli sauce.
7. To prepare the dip sauce, mix all ingredients in a bowl. Serve dim-sums with dip sauce.

Note: For vegetable dumplings, use mixed minced vegetables instead of chicken.

Chilli Paneer with Peppers

Serves 4

1½ tbsp cornflour
1½ tbsp plain flour *(maida)*
½ tsp salt
150 gms paneer
1 green pepper (capsicum) - cut into ¾" pieces
2 tsp soya sauce
2½ tbsp tomato ketchup
½ tbsp vinegar
4-5 green chillies - slit lengthwise
4-5 flakes crushed garlic - optional
1 tbsp coriander - chopped
¼ tsp each of ajinomoto (optional)
¼ tsp each of salt, pepper, sugar
a few tooth picks

1. Mix plain flour, cornflour and salt. Add enough water, about 3 tbsp, to make a batter of a thick pouring consistency, such that it coats the paneer.
2. Cut paneer into ¾" cubes.
3. Dip each piece in the batter and deep fry to a golden brown colour. Keep aside.
4. Heat 2 tbsp oil. Fry the green chillies and garlic. Reduce heat. Add salt, pepper, sugar and ajinomoto.
5. Add soya sauce, chilli sauce, tomato ketchup and vinegar. Stir.
6. Add green peppers. Stir fry for a few seconds.
7. Add the fried paneer and coriander. Mix well. Remove from heat.
8. To serve, thread on a tooth pick - a piece of capsicum, then a paneer and again a piece of capsicum.

Spring Rolls

Picture on facing page *Serves 4*

PANCAKES

½ cup plain flour (maida), 1 cup milk
a pinch of soda-bicarb, ¼ tsp salt
oil for shallow frying

VEGETABLE FILLING

1 onion - chopped finely
8 french beans - parboiled
½ carrot - shredded
½ cup shredded cabbage, ½ cup shredded capsicum
½ cup bean sprouts
a pinch of ajinomoto (optional)
½ tsp white pepper, ½ tsp sugar, salt to taste
1 tsp soya sauce
2 tbsp oil

1. To prepare the pancakes, sift plain flour and salt. Add milk gradually, beating well to make a smooth thin batter. Add soda-bicarb. Mix well.
2. Heat a nonstick pan, taking care not to heat it too much. Smear 1 tsp oil on it.
3. Remove the pan from fire and pour half the batter on it. Tilt the pan to spread the batter evenly. Return to heat.
4. Remove the pancake from the pan when the underside is cooked. Do not cook the other side.
5. Make the other pancake also in the same way. Cool the two pancakes on a dry cloth, keeping the cooked side on top.
6. To prepare the filling, parboil beans. String french beans and drop whole into boiling water with ½ tsp salt for ½ minute. Strain. Then shred diagonally.
7. Heat oil. Add onions and sprouts and stir fry for 1 minute. Add ajinomoto, salt, pepper and sugar.
8. Add all other vegetables. Stir fry for 1 minute. Add soya sauce. Mix.
9. Place half of the filling on the cooked side of the pancake, at one end which is nearest to you.

10. Fold ½" from the left side and then the right side. Roll upwards, holding the sides.
11. Seal edges with cornflour paste, made by dissolving 1 tsp of cornflour in 1 tsp of water. If you chill for ½ hour, it keeps better shape.
12. Heat some oil in a pan. Shallow fry both sides of the roll till golden brown. Drain on absorbent paper. Cut diagonally into 1" pieces. Serve.

CHICKEN SPRING ROLLS

BATTER
1 egg
4 tbsp plain flour (maida), 4 tbsp cornflour
½ cup water, approx., ¼ tsp salt

Prepare a smooth thin batter with the given ingredients. For the filling, **substitute bean sprouts and french beans with 200 gm boiled and shredded chicken.** Saute chicken along with the onions and then add the vegetables as done for vegetable spring rolls.

Vegetable Gold Coin

Picture on page 39   *Serves 12*

6 bread slices
2 small potatoes - boiled
1 spring onion - chopped finely upto the greens (keep greens separate)
1 carrot - chopped finely
1 capsicum - chopped finely
2 tsp soya sauce
½ tsp pepper
¼ tsp chilli powder
¼ tsp ajinomoto (optional)
salt to taste
¼ cup plain flour *(maida)* dissolved in ¼ cup water
1 tbsp white sesame seeds *(til)*
oil for frying

1. Grate boiled potatoes.
2. Heat 1½ tbsp oil. Add only the white part of spring onions. Cook for a minute, till transparent.
3. Add vegetables and the green onions. Cook for 3-4 minutes on low flame.
4. Add potatoes, soya sauce, salt, pepper and chilli powder. Cook for 2-3 minutes. Keep aside.
5. With a cutter or a sharp lid of a bottle, cut out small rounds (about 1½" diameter) of the bread.
6. Spread some potato mixture on the round piece of bread. Press.
7. Spread plain flour paste over the potato mixture.
8. Sprinkle sesame seeds. Press.
9. Deep fry in hot oil. Serve hot, dotted with chilli-garlic sauce.

Soups

Vegetable Stock for Soups

Makes 6 cups

1 onion - chopped
1 carrot - chopped, 1 potato - chopped
4-5 french beans - chopped
or
½ cup chopped cabbage
½ tsp crushed garlic - optional
1 tsp crushed ginger, ½ tsp salt
7 cups water

1. Mix all ingredients and pressure cook for 10-15 minutes.
2. Do not mash the vegetables if a clear soup is to be prepared. Strain and use as required.

Note: Soup cubes or seasoning cubes may be boiled with water and used instead of the stock, if you are short of time.

Chicken Stock for Soups

Makes 10 cups

½ kg chicken - cleaned (keep whole or cut into 8 big pieces)
1 onion - grated or sliced
1 tsp crushed garlic, 1 tsp crushed ginger
1 tsp salt, 12 cups of water

1. Put all the ingredients in a cooker. Pressure cook for 15 minutes.
2. Cool and remove the meat from the bones. (This meat can be used in soups, fried rice, noodles).
3. Add the bones to the liquid in the cooker along with 1 cup of water and cook for another 10 minutes. Strain and use.

Note: Stock can be made in advance and frozen in the freezer compartment and used when required.

Soup cubes or seasoning cubes may be boiled with water and used instead of the stock.

Hot & Sour Chicken Soup

Serves 4

1 breast of chicken - shredded
1 tbsp oil
2 tbsp shredded mushrooms
2 tbsp shredded bamboo shoots (optional)
4 tbsp shredded cabbage
3 tbsp carrot - shredded
leaves of 1 spring onion - finely cut
5 cups chicken stock (page 31)
2 tbsp soya sauce
3 tbsp lime juice or vinegar
1 tsp black pepper
½ tbsp salt
½ tbsp sugar
½ tsp ajinomoto (optional)
4 tbsp cornflour

1 egg - lightly beaten
1 tsp sesame oil or sunflower oil
1 tsp chilli powder

1. Heat 1 tbsp oil in a pan.
2. Add the vegetables (except leaves of spring onions) and saute for a minute.
3. Add the stock and give it 2-3 boils.
4. Reduce heat and add soya sauce, vinegar/lime juice, salt, sugar, ajinomoto and pepper.
5. Add spring onion leaves.
6. Mix cornflour with ½ cup water. Add to the soup, stirring constantly.
7. Bring to a boil. Gradually pour in lightly beaten egg, stirring the soup continuously with a fork to get shreds of egg. Remove from fire.
8. In a spoon heat sesame or sunflower oil and add chilli powder. Add the chilli oil to the soup.
9. Cover soup immediately for a few minutes. Serve hot.

Vegetable Gold Coin: Recipe on page 32 ➤

Hot & Sour Vegetable Soup

Picture on page 2 *Serves 6*

TOMATO STOCK
6 cups water
2 big tomatoes

OTHER INGREDIENTS
2 tbsp oil
1 tomato - chopped very fine
½ cup chopped cabbage
½ cup grated carrot
1 tbsp finely cut french beans
1-2 tbsp dried mushrooms - optional
½ tsp ajinomoto (optional)
½ tsp sugar
1 level tsp black pepper powder
1½ tsp chilli sauce

1½ tbsp vinegar
4 tbsp cornflour mixed with ½ cup water
50 gms tofu or paneer - diced (cut into tiny cubes) - optional

1. Pressure cook water and tomatoes together to give 2-3 whistles. Strain. Keep the tomato stock aside.
2. If dried mushrooms are available, soak them in water for ½ hour to soften.
3. Heat oil. Add chopped tomato. Mince while cooking it. Cook for 1 minute.
4. Add cabbage, carrot, soaked mushrooms and beans. Stir fry for 1 minute.
5. Add the prepared tomato stock.
6. Add all the other ingredients except cornflour paste. Boil for 2 minutes.
7. Add cornflour paste, stirring continuously. Cook for 2-3 minutes till the soup turns thick.
8. Add diced tofu or paneer. Serve hot, accompanied with green chillies in vinegar.

Vegetable Sweet Corn Soup

(with Fresh Corn)

Serves 6

4 big whole corns-on-the cob
½ tsp ajinomoto (optional)
4 level tbsp cornflour dissolved in 1 cup water
2-3 tbsp sugar
salt to taste
½ tsp white pepper
1-2 tbsp white vinegar
½ cup cabbage - shredded
½ cup carrots - very finely chopped

1. Take out a few whole corn kernels and grate the rest of the corn on the grater.
2. Pressure cook corn with 6 cups of water and 2 tsp salt.
3. After the first whistle, keep on low heat for 15 minutes. Remove from heat.
4. After the pressure drops, mix cornflour in water and add to cooked corn.
5. Add sugar, ajinomoto, vinegar and pepper.
6. Give it one boil. Keep it boiling for 8-10 minutes. More cornflour, dissolved in a little water may be added if the soup appears thin.
7. Add the vegetables — cabbage and carrot.
8. After adding the vegetables, boil the soup for 2-3 minutes only. Do not overcook the vegetables, leave them crunchy and crisp.
9. Serve hot with green chillies in vinegar.

Sweet Corn Chicken Soup

Serves 8

10 cups chicken stock (page 36)
1 tin sweet corn (cream style)
1 cup cooked chicken - shredded
3 tbsp cornflour
2 eggs - beaten lightly
salt and pepper to taste
1 tsp sugar
½ tsp ajinomoto (optional)

1. Pour stock into a pan. Mix in the sweet corn and allow to cook on high heat for 5-7 minutes.
2. Add sugar, ajinomoto, salt and pepper.
3. Mix cornflour in ½ cup water, add to the soup stirring all the time until the soup gets thick.
4. Add the beaten eggs and stir with a fork so that threads are formed.
5. Add the shredded and cooked chicken pieces, keeping a little aside to sprinkle on top of the soup when poured into the bowls.
6. Serve hot along with soya sauce, green chillies in vinegar and chilli sauce.

Chicken Talumein Soup

4 cups chicken stock - recipe on page 36
½ cup cooked shredded chicken
½ carrot - parboiled and cut into leaves or diagonally cut slices
1-2 cabbage leaves - roughly torn
½ cup boiled noodles
2 tbsp cornflour dissolved in ½ cup water
1½ tsp soya sauce
salt to taste
½ tsp each of sugar, black pepper
a pinch ajinomoto (optional)

1. Mix stock, salt, pepper, sugar, soya sauce and ajinomoto. Boil.
2. Add cornflour paste, stirring continuously.
3. Add vegetables and shredded chicken.
4. Boil for 2-3 minutes.
5. Add boiled noodles, remove from fire. Serve.

Chicken, Mutton & Seafood

Chicken in Black Pepper Sauce

Picture on back cover *Serves 4*

200 gm chicken (boneless) - cut into 1" pieces
greens of 1 spring onion - cut into ½" pieces

SAUCE
½ tsp peppercorns (saboot kali mirch)
½ tsp chopped garlic, ½ tsp ginger paste
1 tsp freshly ground black pepper
½ - 1 tsp soya sauce
pinch of ajinomoto
1½ tbsp cornflour
1 tsp vinegar
2 tbsp oil

1½ cups water mixed with 1 chicken seasoning cube
OR 1½ cups chicken stock

MARINADE
1 egg, ½ tsp salt, ¼ tsp ajinomoto (optional)
1 tbsp cornflour, 1 tbsp oil

1. Cut chicken into 1" pieces.
2. Marinate the chicken in all the ingredients of the marinade and keep aside for atleast ½ hour.
3. Heat 4 tbsp oil in a wok or a kadhai and stir fry the chicken for 3-4 minutes on medium heat. Drain and keep aside.
4. For the sauce, heat 2 tbsp oil. Reduce heat, add ginger, garlic and peppercorns. Cook till garlic changes colour. Add black pepper, soya sauce, ajinomoto, vinegar and chicken. Add water mixed with cube or chicken stock. Cook till chicken turns tender. Add enough water (½ cup approx.) mixed with cornflour. Cook stirring till it turns to a thick saucy consistency.
5. Add vinegar & greens of spring onion. Remove from fire. Serve hot.

Chicken in Hot Garlic Sauce

Serves 4

200 gms chicken breast boneless
1 tbsp chopped garlic
2 tsp red chilli paste
1½ tbsp tomato ketchup
salt - to taste
¼ tsp ajinomoto (optional)
1 tsp sugar
1/3 cup chicken stock (page 31)
1 tbsp cornflour
4 tbsp oil
1 tsp vinegar
1 tbsp capsicum - cut into tiny cubes (diced)
1 tbsp onions - finely chopped
2 tsp spring onions - finely chopped

MARINADE
1 egg
¾ tsp salt
¼ tsp ajinomoto (optional)
1 tbsp cornflour
1 tbsp oil

1. Cut the chicken breast into even sized pieces.
2. Marinate the chicken in all the ingredients of the marinade and keep aside.
3. Heat 4 tbsp oil in a wok and stir-fry the chicken for 2-3 minutes. Drain and keep aside.
4. To the oil remaining in the wok, add garlic and chilli paste. When garlic changes colour, add tomato ketchup.
5. Add the capsicum, onion and spring onion. Stir-fry for 1 minute.
6. Add chicken. Stir-fry and add salt, ajinomoto, sugar and stock.
7. Dissolve cornflour in 2 tbsp of water and add to the chicken. Thicken the sauce, stirring continuously. Finish with vinegar.
8. Serve hot along with boiled rice or noodles.

Chicken Manchurian

Serves 4

½ chicken - cut into 1" square pieces

EGG BATTER
1 egg
1½ tbsp cornflour
1½ tbsp plain flour *(maida)*
salt & pepper to taste

MANCHURIAN SAUCE
2 tbsp oil
2 tbsp crushed ginger
2 tbsp crushed garlic
2 tbsp crushed green chillies
2 tbsp chopped coriander
1 cup chicken stock (page 36) or 1 cup water mixed with 1 chicken seasoning cube

1 tsp sherry - optional
1 tbsp soya sauce
¼ tsp salt
¼ tsp pepper
¼ tsp sugar
¼ tsp ajinomoto (optional)
2-3 tbsp cornflour dissolved in ¼ cup water

1. Mix all ingredients of the batter.
2. Dip the chicken pieces in the batter, deep fry till golden brown. Keep aside.
3. For the manchurian sauce, heat oil in a wok . Lightly fry garlic and ginger till they just change colour.
4. Add green chillies and coriander leaves. Mix.
5. Reduce heat, add chicken stock, soya sauce, sherry, salt, sugar, pepper and ajinomoto. Cook for 2-3 minutes.
6. Add cornflour mixed with water and give one boil. Add fried chicken and cook for 1-2 minutes. Serve hot.

Spicy Honey Chicken

Picture on page 103 *Serves 4*

250 gm chicken breast boneless
½ cup cornflour - approx.
2-3 dry, red chillies - broken into bits
2 tsp garlic paste
2 tbsp spring onions - white part finely chopped and greens cut into 1" pieces
2½ tbsp tomato ketchup
1½-2 tbsp soya sauce
2 tsp honey
oil for frying

MARINADE
2 eggs
½ tsp salt, ½ tsp ajinomoto (optional)
1 tbsp cornflour
1 tbsp oil

1. Cut the chicken breast into even slices.
2. Mix all the ingredients of the marinade and marinate the chicken and keep aside for 1 hour.
3. Coat the marinated chicken with dry cornflour. See to it that each piece is coated.
4. Deep fry the chicken till crisp & golden brown. Drain and keep aside.
5. Heat 2 tbsp oil in a wok.
6. Reduce heat. Add dry, red chillies and stir. Add garlic paste. Stir for a few seconds.
7. Add finely chopped white part of spring onions, tomato ketchup, soya sauce and honey. Saute for a few seconds.
8. Add the crispy fried chicken and stir-fry ensuring that each piece is coated with the sauce. Mix in the greens of spring onions. Serve hot.

Crispy Fried Fish

Serves 2

1 whole pomfret
1 tsp salt
3 tbsp rice wine
a pinch of ajinomoto (optional)
3 tbsp cornflour
oil for frying
1½ tbsp finely chopped spring onions

SAUCE
¼ cup oil
1½ tsp finely chopped ginger
1½ tbsp sugar
¼ tsp pepper
3 tbsp vinegar
1/3 cup tomato ketchup

Spicy Honey Vegetables: Recipe on page 71 ➢

1. Make slanting slashes all down both sides of fish about ¾" apart. Repeat in opposite direction.
2. Mix salt, rice wine and 1½ tbsp cornflour in a shallow dish, large enough to contain the fish. Roll fish in this mixture turning the sides. Leave to stand for 15 minutes.
3. Heat about ½ cup oil over high heat. Reduce heat. Add fish and fry over moderate heat. Remove and place in a dish.
4. To prepare the sauce, in a saucepan heat ¼ cup fresh oil and stir fry finely chopped spring onions and ginger for a few seconds.
5. Add sugar, vinegar, pepper and ketchup and cook to reduce & thicken.
6. Pour the sauce over the cooked fish.

Dry Chilli Chicken

Serves 6

500 gms chicken - cut into 2" bite size pieces (if desired it can be boneless)
6-8 green chillies - slit lengthwise
3 tbsp oil
1-2 spring onions - cut into ½" pieces

MARINADE
2 tbsp ginger-garlic paste
4 tbsp soya sauce, 1 tbsp vinegar, 1 tsp red chilli powder
1 tsp sugar, ½ tsp ajinomoto (optional), ½ tsp salt
2 tbsp sherry - optional

1. Marinate the chicken pieces in the marinade for at least 2 hours.
2. Heat oil. Fry green chillies lightly and remove. Add the marinated chicken pieces along with the marinade. Fry well till it dries up.
3. Mix in the green chillies and serve sprinkled with spring onions.

Pork or Mince Meat Balls

Serves 6

BALLS

1½ cups ground or finely chopped pork or lamb
1 spring onion - finely chopped
2 thin slices ginger - finely chopped
2 flakes garlic - crushed and chopped
½ tsp salt
½ tsp sugar
2-3 tbsp soya sauce
2 tsp sesame oil
2 tbsp rice wine
¼ tsp pepper
½ tsp ajinomoto (optional)
¼ cup cornflour
¼ cup plain flour *(maida)*
1-2 green chillies - finely chopped

OTHER INGREDIENTS
2 eggs - lightly beaten
½ cup cornflour
oil for frying

1. Thoroughly mix all ingredients listed in the ingredients for the balls.
2. Shape this mixture into small balls.
3. Dip in lightly beaten eggs & roll in cornflour to coat. Shake off excess.
4. Heat oil in a wok and fry the meat balls until golden brown all over.
5. Serve hot along with chilli sauce.

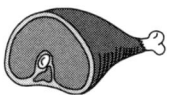

Mongolian Chicken

A semi dry sweet and sour chicken in a Chinese red sauce.

Picture on page 1   Serves 4

200 gm chicken - cut into bite size (1½ - 2") pieces
3 tbsp tomato ketchup
1 tbsp vinegar
½ tsp ajinomoto
1 cup water mixed with 1 chicken seasoning cube or ½ cup chicken stock
4 tbsp oil
2 spring onions - white part finely chopped & greens of onions cut into 1" pieces
2 tbsp cornflour
1 tsp chilli powder
10 flakes garlic - crushed
3 tbsp coriander

MARINADE
1 egg, ½ tsp salt, ½ tsp pepper, ¼ tsp ajinomoto (optional)
1 tbsp cornflour, 1 tbsp oil, a pinch of orange colour

1. Cut chicken into 1" pieces.
2. Marinate the chicken in all the ingredients of the marinade and keep aside for atleast ½ hour.
3. Heat 4 tbsp oil in a wok or a kadhai and stir fry the chicken for 3-4 minutes on medium heat till cooked. Drain and keep aside.
4. In a frying pan heat 2 tbsp oil reduce heat add chilli powder.
5. Add crushed garlic, fry a little and add chicken pieces. Remove the chicken from the pan.
6. To the remaining oil add green spring onions and fry for a minute.
7. Add water mixed with seasoning cube or chicken stock. Boil.
8. Add tomato ketchup, ajinomoto and sugar. Add salt to taste. Boil for a minute.
9. Dissolve cornflour in ½ cup water and add to the stock, stirring continuously till the sauce thickens.
10. Add the chicken, green part of spring onions and chopped coriander cook for 1 minute. Add vinegar and remove from fire. Serve hot.

Honeyed Shrimps

Serves 4

750 gm shrimps - peeled with tail intact
3 tbsp oil
1 clove garlic - crushed
1" piece ginger - finely chopped
¼ cup honey
2 tsp soya sauce
a few sesame seeds *(til)*

1. Heat oil in a wok. Add garlic and ginger and stir-fry for 30 seconds.
2. Add shrimp in two batches and stir-fry until pink. Remove the first batch before cooking the second.
3. Add honey and soya sauce and toss quickly. Serve sprinkled with sesame seeds.

Vegetable Dishes

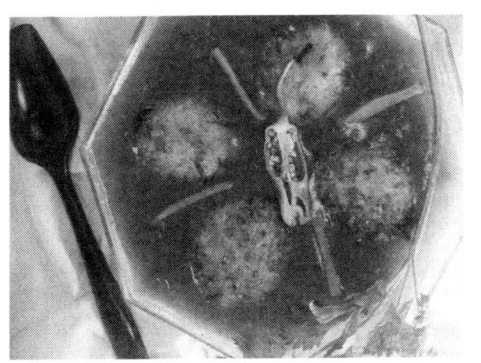

Vegetables in Ginger Garlic Sauce with Sesame Seeds

Serves 4

1 small carrot - parboiled & cut into round slices
¼ of a small cauliflower or broccoli - cut into small flat florets and parboiled
1 small onion - cut into 4 pieces and separated
4-5 button mushrooms or dried mushrooms
4-6 baby corns, 1 capsicum - cut into ½" cubes
50 gm cabbage - cut into 1" squares

SAUCE

6-8 flakes garlic - crushed, 1 tbsp ginger paste
2 tbsp tomato ketchup, 1 tsp soya sauce, 2 tsp vinegar
2-3 tbsp oil
½ tsp white pepper, ½ tsp salt, or to taste, ¼ tsp sugar
1½ tbsp cornflour mixed with 1 cup water
1 tbsp sesame seeds

1. To parboil vegetables, boil 4 cups water with ½ tsp salt. Peel the carrot and drop the whole carrot and cauliflower florets in boiling water. Let them boil for 2-3 minutes. Remove from water. Cut carrots into ¼" thick round slices.
2. Cut capsicum into ½" pieces. Trim mushrooms, cut onions into fours and separate the slices.
3. Dissolve cornflour in 1 cup water and keep aside.
4. Heat 1½ tbsp oil in a kadhai. Reduce heat and add ginger and ½ of garlic paste. Fry till changes colour.
5. Add baby corns, carrots, cauliflower, onion and mushrooms. Stir for 4-5 minutes. Add capsicum. Add salt and pepper. Mix and remove the vegetables. Keep aside.
6. In the same kadhai heat 1 tbsp oil. Add sesame seeds, wait till golden. Add the left over garlic, stir till it changes colour. Reduce heat.
7. Add cornflour paste and cook stirring continuously till sauce turns thick.
8. At serving time mix in stir fried vegetables and serve immediately. Serve sprinkled with 1 tsp of toasted sesame seeds.

Note: Toast sesame seeds on a tawa (griddle) till golden.

Cubed Paneer & Veg Sizzler

Serves 2

100 gms paneer - cut into ½" cubes
6 mushrooms - cut into halves, 1 small onion - cut into 4 pieces and separated
1 carrot - cut into small cubes and boiled
½ capsicum - cut into ½" pieces,
1 slice of tinned pineapple - cut into small pieces
½ tsp salt and ½ tsp freshly crushed pepper, or to taste
2 tbsp oil

SAUCE
2 tbsp oil
6-7 flakes garlic - crushed
2 green chillies - deseeded & chopped finely
½ tbsp soya sauce, a few drops tabasco or capsico sauce
1 tbsp red chilli sauce, 3 tbsp tomato ketchup
1 tbsp vinegar, ¼ tsp pepper and ½ tsp salt, or to taste
2 level tbsp cornflour dissolved in 1½ cups water

TO SERVE
2 tbsp butter
a sizzler plate, rice boiled with salt and lemon juice

1. Heat 2 tbsp oil in a non-stick pan or kadhai. Add mushrooms. Saute till light brown and dry. Add onion. Saute for 2 minutes. Add carrots. Stir for 1-2 minutes.
2. Add capsicum, pineapple and paneer. Add salt and freshly crushed pepper. Cook for 1 minute. Remove all vegetables and paneer from the kadhai and keep aside.
3. To prepare the sauce, heat 2 tbsp oil in a clean kadhai. Reduce heat. Add garlic and green chillies. Stir for a few seconds on low heat till garlic just changes colour.
4. Remove from fire. Add all sauces and vinegar. Cook on slow fire for a few seconds. Add salt and pepper to taste. Add cornflour paste, stirring continuously till a sauce is ready. Add vegetables and paneer. Cook for 1 minute on low heat.

contd...

5. To serve, remove the iron sizzler plate from the wooden base. Heat the iron plate by keeping it directly on the flame. Reduce heat and let the iron plate be on fire while it is being filled. Put 2-3 tbsp water in the wooden base and scatter 1 tbsp butter cut into pieces on the wooden base. Keep wooden base aside.
6. When the iron plate is heated, scatter 1 tbsp butter here and there. Place 2-3 cabbage leaves on the plate and arrange rice on it. Leave on slow flame for 2 minutes for the rice to get heated. Put the hot vegetables in sauce in the centre portion of the rice. When the hot sauce falls on the hot plate, it sizzles. With the help of a firm pair of tongs (sansi), place the iron plate on the on the wooden tray. Serve sizzling hot.

Spicy Honey Vegetables

Picture on page 57 *Serves 4*

1 small carrot - parboiled and cut into round slices
½ cup cauliflower or broccoli - cut into small, flat florets (¼ of a small flower)
1 small onion - cut into 4 pieces and separated
4-5 mushrooms
4-6 baby corns (optional)
1 capsicum - cut into ½" cubes
1 tbsp soya sauce, 2 tsp chilli sauce, 1½ tbsp tomato sauce
2 tsp honey
½ tbsp vinegar
¼ tsp freshly ground pepper, 1 tsp salt, or to taste
a pinch ajinomoto (optional)
3 tbsp cornflour mixed with ¼ cup water
2-3 tbsp oil
3-4 dried, red chillies - broken into small pieces
8-10 flakes garlic - crushed

1. To parboil carrot, boil 4 cups water with 1 tsp salt. Peel the carrot and drop the whole carrot in boiling water. Let it boil for 2-3 minutes. Remove from water. Cut carrots into ¼" thick round slices or flowers.
2. Cut capsicum into ½" pieces. Break cauliflower or broccoli into small florets and cut each floret into two. Trim mushrooms and baby corns, keeping them whole. Cut onion into fours and separate the slices.
3. Dissolve cornflour in ¼ cup water and keep aside.
4. Heat oil in a kadhai. Reduce heat and add broken red chillies and garlic.
5. Stir and add baby corns, carrots, cauliflower, onion and mushrooms. Stir for 4-5 minutes. Add capsicum. Add salt & pepper.
6. Stir and add chilli sauce, tomato sauce, soya sauce, honey and vinegar. Pour 2 cups of water and bring to a boil. Lower heat and simmer for ½ minute.
7. Add the dissolved cornflour and cook till the vegetables get done and the sauce turns thick.
8. Spread the warm rice in a serving plate. Pour the hot vegetables over the rice and serve immediately.

Vegetable Manchurian

Picture on page 75   *Serves 6*

MANCHURIAN BALLS
1 cup grated cauliflower
¼ cup diced or grated carrots
¼ cup finely grated cabbage
1-2 slices bread - dipped in water and squeezed
1 tbsp cornflour, 1 tbsp flour (maida)
¼ tsp ajinomoto, salt and pepper to taste, 2-3 tbsp milk

MANCHURIAN SAUCE
2 tbsp oil
1" piece ginger - crushed to a paste, 5-6 flakes garlic - crushed - optional
2 green chillies - chopped, ½ onion - very finely chopped
1 tbsp soya sauce, 1½ tbsp tomato ketchup, 2 tsp vinegar
½ tsp salt, ¼ tsp pepper
1½ - 2 tbsp cornflour - dissolved in ½ cup water
1 spring onion greens - chopped finely, to garnish

1. Mix all ingredients of the balls, adding only 1 slice of bread first. (More bread may be added if balls fall apart on frying.) Add enough milk so that the balls bind together easily. Make oval balls. Flatten each ball.
2. Deep fry 3-4 pieces at a time on medium flame. Reduce flame after the balls turn light brown and fry till cooked and brown. Keep aside.
3. To prepare manchurian sauce, heat 2 tbsp oil. Add ginger and garlic. Fry on low flame for 1 minute.
4. Add green chillies and onions. Cook till they turn light brown.
5. Reduce heat and add soya sauce, tomato sauce, vinegar, salt and pepper. Cook for 2-3 minutes.
6. Add 1½ cups of water. Boil. Keep on slow fire for 2-3 minutes.
7. Dissolve cornflour in ½ cup water and add to the above sauce, stirring continuously. Cook till slightly thick. Keep the sauce aside.
8. To serve, boil the sauce. Add the balls to the manchurian sauce and keep on slow fire for one minute till the balls are heated through. Serve hot sprinkled with finely chopped spring onion greens with fried rice or noodles.

Vegetable Manchurian: Recipe on page 73 ➢

Baby Corns in Ginger Sauce

Serves 4

200 gm baby corns - cut into 1" pieces
3 tbsp oil
¼ tsp ajinomoto (optional)
1 tbsp ginger paste
1 tsp finely chopped ginger
1 tsp salt & ½ tsp pepper, or to taste
3 tsp soya sauce
3 tbsp tomato ketchup
½ tsp sugar
2 tbsp cornflour dissolved in 1½ cups water
1 spring onion greens - cut into 1" pieces

1. Heat 2 tbsp oil in a wok. Add baby corns.
2. Add ¼ tsp salt and ajinomoto.
3. Stir fry for 2-3 minutes till cooked. Remove from wok and keep aside.
4. Heat 1 tbsp more of oil. Add chopped ginger. Stir till ginger turns golden brown. Add ginger paste. Cook on low flame for ½ minute.
5. Add the spring onion greens.
6. Add ¾ tsp salt and ½ tsp pepper. Stir fry for a few seconds.
7. Reduce heat. Add soya sauce, tomato ketchup and sugar. Cook for ½ minute.
8. Add the stir fried baby corns. Stir to mix well.
9. Add the cornflour paste, stirring continuously. Cook till the sauce turns thick and it coats the baby corns.

Cantonese Vegetables

Serves 8

½ cabbage - cut into big chunks
2 medium sized carrots - parboiled & cut into thick rounds
2 medium sized onions - cut into fours
1 capsicum - cut into 8 pieces
1 small cucumber - cut into rounds
2 cups water
2 tbsp soya sauce
1 tbsp chilli sauce
1 tbsp vinegar
1 tsp pepper
salt to taste
¼ tsp ajinomoto (optional)
1 tsp sugar
2 - 3 tbsp cornflour dissolved in water

1. Wash and cut vegetables into big pieces.
2. Stir fry each vegetable separately in little oil.
3. Do not over fry. The colour of the vegetables should not change.
4. Take out the vegetables into a serving dish.
5. Heat 1 tbsp oil. Add soya sauce, chilli sauce, vinegar, salt, pepper, ajinomoto and sugar. Stir on low heat for a few seconds.
6. Add water. Boil.
7. Add cornflour paste, stirring continuously. Remove from fire when thick.
8. Add the vegetables to the sauce and serve hot.

Vegetable HongKong
with Fried Noodles

Serves 4

3-4 medium florets of cauliflower - parboiled
1 carrot - cut into leaves - parboiled, 5-6 french beans - parboiled
2-3 leaves of cabbage - torn into big pieces
1 capsicum - cut into big pieces
1 spring onion - quartered
1 tsp finely chopped garlic or ginger
2-3 dry red chillies - broken into pieces
¼ pinches ajinomoto (optional), ½ tsp sugar, salt and pepper to taste
2 tbsp soya sauce, 2 tsp vinegar, 2 tsp chilli sauce
1½ tbsp cornflour dissolved in 1 cup water
3 tbsp oil
2-3 tbsp walnuts or cashewnuts

FRIED NOODLES

2 cups boiled noodles, 2 tbsp oil, ½ tsp salt, ¼ tsp ajinomoto (optional)
¼ tsp red chilli powder, 1 tbsp soya sauce

1. Heat 3 tbsp oil in a wok or a frying pan. Reduce heat. Add nuts. Fry to a golden colour on low flame. Remove from pan.
2. Add ginger or garlic to the oil. Cook for ½ minute.
3. Add red chillies, vegetables and ajinomoto. Stir fry over a high flame for 2 minutes.
4. Add the soya sauce, vinegar, chilli sauce, salt, pepper and sugar.
5. Add cornflour paste, stirring continuously. Cook till the sauce thickens and coats the vegetables. Keep aside.
6. To prepare the fried noodles, heat 2 tbsp oil in a clean wok. Reduce heat. Add salt, ajinomoto and chilli powder. Mix. Add soya sauce and stir for a few seconds. Add boiled noodles. Fry turning occasionally, till the noodles are evenly browned.
7. Add more soya sauce if a darker colour is desired. Remove from fire.
8. To serve, place the vegetables in the centre of a plate and surround them with fried noodles. Garnish the vegetables with fried nuts.

Rice & Noodles

Vegetable Fried Rice

Serves 4

1½ cups uncooked rice - boiled and spread on a tray to dry
2 tbsp oil
2 green chillies - chopped finely, 2 flakes garlic - crushed & chopped (optional)
2 green onions - chopped, keep greens separate
¼ cup very finely sliced french beans, 1 carrot - finely diced
½ big capsicum - diced
salt, pepper, ajinomoto (optional) - ½ tsp of each
1-2 tsp soya sauce (according to the colour desired), 1 tsp vinegar (optional)

1. Heat oil. Stir fry garlic, green chillies and white of onions.
2. Add beans, then carrots. Stir fry for 1 minute. Add capsicum.
3. Add salt, pepper and ajinomoto.
4. Add rice. Add soya sauce, vinegar and chilli sauce.
5. Add green onions and salt to taste. Stir fry the rice for 2 minutes. Serve hot.

Haka Noodles with Vegetables

Serves 4

FRIED NOODLES

100 gm noodles - boiled
2 tbsp oil
3 dry whole red chillies - broken into bits
½ tsp chilli powder, 2 tsp soya sauce, ½ tsp salt

VEGETABLES

1 capsicum - shredded, 1 carrot - shredded
½ cup shredded cabbage
3-4 flakes garlic - crushed and chopped (optional)
2-3 spring onions or 1 ordinary onion
2 tbsp shredded bamboo shoots - optional
3-4 tbsp bean sprouts - optional, 1-2 tbsp dried mushrooms
½ tsp each of salt & pepper, ½ tsp sugar, ½ tsp ajinomoto (optional)
1 tbsp soya sauce, 2 tsp vinegar
1 cup water, 1½ tbsp cornflour dissolved in ½ cup water

1. In a pan, heat 2 tbsp oil. Remove from fire, add broken red chillies and chilli powder.
2. Return to fire and mix in the boiled noodles, salt and soya sauce. Fry for 1 minute, till evenly brown in colour.
3. Keep the fried noodles aside.
4. To prepare the vegetables, shred all vegetables.
5. Heat 3 tbsp oil. Reduce heat and add garlic.
6. Add vegetables in sequence of their tenderness - onions, sprouts, bamboo shoots, capsicum, carrot and cabbage.
7. Add ajinomoto, salt and pepper. Add soya sauce and vinegar. Cook for ½ minute.
8. Add water. Boil.
9. Add cornflour mixture, stirring continuously. Cook for 1 minute till thick. Remove from fire.
10. To serve, spread the fried noodles on a platter.
11. Pour the prepared hot vegetables over the noodles. Serve.

Chicken Fried Rice

Serves 4

1 cup uncooked rice
3 tbsp oil
1 onion - finely chopped, 2 green chillies - chopped
½ tsp ajinomoto (optional)
¼ of a cabbage - thinly sliced and chopped finely
1 carrot - finely chopped
½ cup boiled, shredded chicken
½ tsp pepper powder, 2 tsp salt, ½ tsp sugar
2-3 tsp soya sauce
2 spring onions - diced

1. Wash rice. Soak in water for half an hour. Cook in chicken stock or water.
2. When the rice gets done, strain and spread on a tray. Cool under a fan. Rice should remain separate.
3. Heat oil in a wok and fry onions till very light brown. Add green chillies and ajinomoto. Add cabbage and carrot. Stir fry for 1-2 minutes.
4. Add boiled shredded chicken. Saute for a minute. Add salt and sugar.
5. Add 2-3 tsp soya sauce. Mix well. Add rice. Mix well. Add pepper powder.
6. Add spring onions. Mix well, stir fry for a few seconds and remove from fire. Serve hot.

American Chopsuey

Serves 4

1 carrot - parboiled, 8 french beans - parboiled
1 green chilli - shredded, 1 capsicum - shredded, 1 onion - shredded
¾ cup shredded cabbage
½ cup bean sprouts
2 cups water
5 tbsp oil
¼ tsp ajinomoto (optional), ½ tsp white pepper, salt to taste
4 tbsp tomato ketchup, 1 tsp vinegar , 1 tsp soya sauce
3 tbsp cornflour dissolved in ½ cup water

CRISPY NOODLES
100 gms noodles
oil for deep frying

1. To prepare crispy noodles, deep fry the noodles in two batches, in hot smoking oil until crisp and golden brown. Keep aside.
2. Scrape carrot, string french beans.
3. Parboil them by dropping the whole carrot and french beans in 2 cups of boiling water with ½ tsp salt. Strain after half a minute. Cool.
4. Shred all vegetables - capsicum, onion, cabbage, carrot and french beans.
5. Heat 5 tbsp of oil. Add sprouts and ajinomoto. Stir fry for 1 minute.
6. Add the chicken if using. Add remaining vegetables, pepper and salt. Stir fry for 2 minutes.
7. Add soya sauce, vinegar and tomato ketchup. Cook for ½ minute.
8. Add water. Bring to a boil. Add cornflour paste, stirring continuously. Cook for about 2 minutes, till thick. Keep aside.
9. To serve, spread crispy noodles on a serving platter, keeping aside a few for the top.
10. Top with the prepared vegetables. Sprinkle some left over crispy noodles on it. Serve hot.

Vegetable Chow Mein

Serves 4

100 gm noodles
2-3 flakes garlic - crushed (optional)
1 onion - shredded
1 capsicum - shredded
1 cup shredded cabbage
1 carrot - shredded
¼ tsp ajinomoto (optional)
1 tsp white pepper
a pinch sugar
2 tsp soya sauce
1 tbsp vinegar
1½ tsp chilli sauce
2 tbsp oil
¾ tsp salt

1. Boil noodles and dry them by spreading them on a big tray.
2. Shred all vegetables into thin long strips. To shred onions, peel and cut into half. Cut each half into thin semi circles to get thin long strips of onion.
4. Heat oil. Add garlic. Add onions. Stir fry for ½ minute.
5. Stir fry carrots and capsicum for ½ minute. Add cabbage.
6. Add salt, pepper, sugar and ajinomoto.
7. Add boiled noodles. Add soya sauce and mix well.
8. Add vinegar and chilli sauce. Stir fry for 1 minute. Add more soya sauce for a darker colour. Serve.

Chicken Haka Noodles

Serves 4

3 tbsp oil
1 tsp chilli powder
4-5 flakes garlic - crushed
200 gms shredded chicken
2-3 spring onions - shredded diagonally
3-4 tbsp bean sprouts , 2 tbsp shredded bamboo
1 tbsp shredded mushrooms
1 capsicum - shredded, 1 medium sized carrot - shredded
50 gms cabbage - shredded
2 tbsp soya sauce, 2 tsp vinegar
1 cup chicken stock
½ tsp each of salt, sugar & pepper
½ tsp ajinomoto (optional)
1-2 tbsp cornflour dissolved in ½ cup water

Toffee Apples: Recipe on page 98 ➢

NOODLES

100 gms noodles
½ tsp chilli powder, ½ tsp salt
2 dried red chillies, 2 tsp soya sauce, 3-4 tbsp oil

1. Shred vegetables. In a frying pan, heat 3 tbsp oil, reduce heat and add chilli powder. Add garlic. Add the chicken pieces. Fry to a pale colour.
2. Add onion, bean sprouts, bamboo shoots, mushrooms, capsicum, carrot and then cabbage. Stir fry for 1-2 minutes. Reduce heat and add the stock and all the other ingredients, except cornflour paste.
3. Give one boil and add cornflour paste. Cook till the sauce turns thick. Remove from fire and keep aside.
4. To boil the noodles, boil 5-6 cups water with 1 tsp salt. Boil the noodles in salted water for 3-4 minutes. Drain the water. Put the noodles under running water. Rub a little oil over the noodles. Spread on a tray to cool.
5. In a frying pan heat oil, reduce heat, add broken chillies and then chilli powder. Mix in the boiled noodles. Add salt and soya sauce. Stir fry for 2 minutes.
6. To serve, put noodles on a platter. Pour warm vegetables over it.

American Chicken Chopsuey

Serves 4

2 tbsp oil
2 flakes of garlic - crushed
2-3 spring onions - chopped
2-3 mushrooms - shredded
3 tbsp bean sprouts
1 medium sized carrot - shredded
6-7 tbsp shredded cabbage
50 gms each of shredded chicken, prawns and ham (increase quantity of the other two if omitting any one)
¼ tsp each of salt and ajinomoto (optional), ½ tsp sugar
2 tbsp soya sauce
4 tbsp tomato ketchup
1 tsp sherry/gin
1 cup chicken stock or 1 seasoning cube dissolved in 1 cup water
3 tsp cornflour

TOPPING
1 egg - fried

CRISPY NOODLES
100 gms chow noodles
oil for deep frying

1. Deep fry the noodles in two batches, in hot smoking oil until crisp and golden brown. Keep aside.
2. In a wok, heat oil, saute garlic. Add chicken, ham and prawns.
3. Fry to a pale colour. Stir fry in sequence - spring onions, bean sprouts, bamboo shoots, carrot, cabbage. Reduce heat.
4. Add chicken stock, sauces and seasonings. Cook for 2 minutes.
5. Mix cornflour with water and add to make a thick sauce. Further cook for 2-3 minutes till thick.
6. In a serving dish, put the crispy noodles (noodles fried in oil). Pour the meat & vegetables on the crispy noodles. Place a fried egg on top.
7. Serve hot garnished with chopped spring onions.

Desserts

Toffee Apples

Picture on page 93   *Serves 4*

3 delicious golden or red apples
½ cup plain flour *(maida)*
2 tbsp cornflour
½ tsp baking powder

CARAMEL COATING
1 cup sugar
2 tbsp oil, ½ cup water
2 tsp sesame (*til*) seeds
oil for deep frying

1. Put the sugar, 2 tbsp oil and ½ cup of water in a pan and cook on a high flame.
2. When the mixture begins to bubble, stir continuously to prevent the sugar from burning.

3. Continue stirring the pan until the syrup is light brown in colour and feels sticky when felt between the thumb and the fore finger. It forms a thread when the finger is pulled apart.
4. Remove from the heat, add the sesame seeds and mix well. Keep the caramel syrup aside.
5. Mix the plain flour, cornflour and baking powder in a bowl. Add enough water to get a smooth, thick batter of a coating consistency.
6. Peel and cut the apples into four pieces. Remove the seeds.
7. Heat oil for frying. Coat the apple pieces evenly with the batter and deep fry 5-6 pieces together at one time, in hot oil until golden.
8. Keep a serving bowl filled with ice-cubes ready and cover with water.
9. Put the fried apples in the caramel syrup and coat evenly. Drain well and dip immediately into the ice-cubes bowl. Keep for a few minutes till the caramel coating hardens.
10. Drain thoroughly. Keep aside till serving time.
11. Serve plain or with ice cream.

Note: You may use pears or babugoshas too.

Date & Coconut Pancakes

Serves 4

½ cup cornflour
½ cup plain flour (*maida*)
½ cup milk
1 cup water, approx.
1 tbsp sesame seeds (*til*)
2 tsp melted butter or oil
a pinch salt
oil for frying

FILLING
½ cup grated fresh coconut
½ cup dates - deseeded and finely chopped
¼ cup powdered sugar

TO SERVE
vanilla ice-cream

1. Mix all ingredients of the filling together and keep aside.
2. Mix the cornflour, plain flour, butter and salt in a bowl. Add milk. Add water gradually to get a thin pouring batter of a smooth consistency. Add sesame seeds and mix well.
3. Put 1 tsp oil onto a nonstick frying pan of about 7" diameter and keep on fire.
4. Do not make the pan too hot. Pour 1 small *karchhi*, (about 2 tbsp) of the batter in the pan and shake the pan in a circular motion so as to spread the batter evenly.
5. Cook firstly on one side until done and then on the other side.
6. Repeat with the remaining batter.
7. To serve, spread 1 tbsp of the filling on each pancake and fold. If desired, seal the edges by applying a little of the pancake mixture.
8. Fry until crisp. Cut into pieces and serve with vanilla ice cream.

Almond Float

Serves 4

2½ cups milk
¼ cup sugar
a few drops almond extract
2 tbsp gelatine
½ cup water
some fresh fruits and canned lychees

1. Heat milk, remove from heat and add sugar. Cool slightly then add almond extract; cool.
2. Sprinkle gelatine over water and leave until water is absorbed. Dissolve gelatine over low heat and cool. Stir into milk mixture. Chill till set.
3. When ready to serve, cut almond gelatine into diamond shapes. Place fruit in a serving bowl and arrange diamond shapes on top.

Spicy Honey Chicken: Recipe on page 54 ➤

BEST SELLERS BY *Nita Mehta*

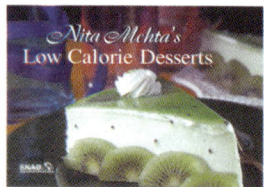
Low Calorie Desserts

CONTINENTAL-NV

Punjabi Cooking

Taste of KASHMIR

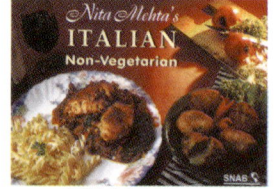
ITALIAN-NV

OVEN Recipes-NV

Taste of RAJASTHAN

The Best of MUTTON

MORE CHICKEN

Great Ideas - Cooking Tips

LOSE WEIGHT

SANDWICHES